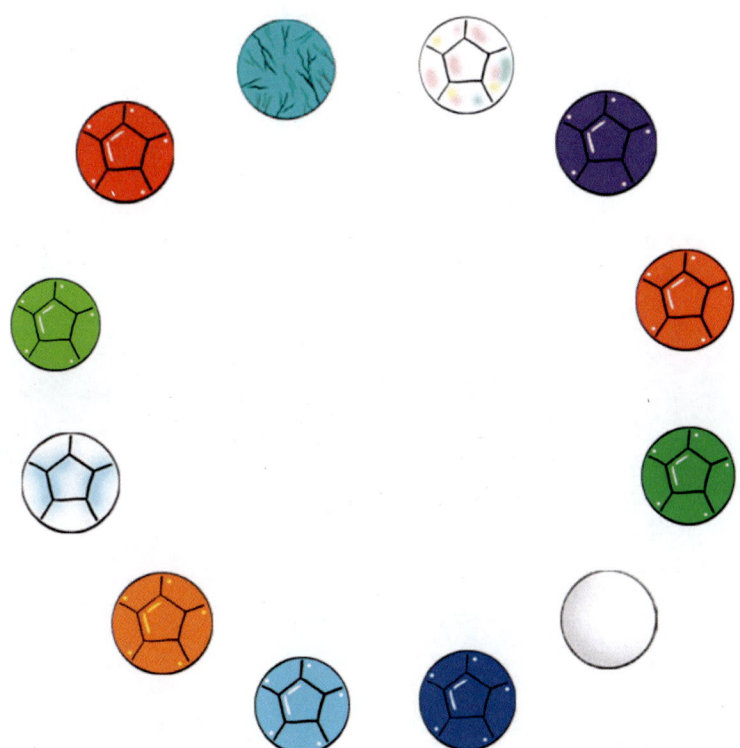

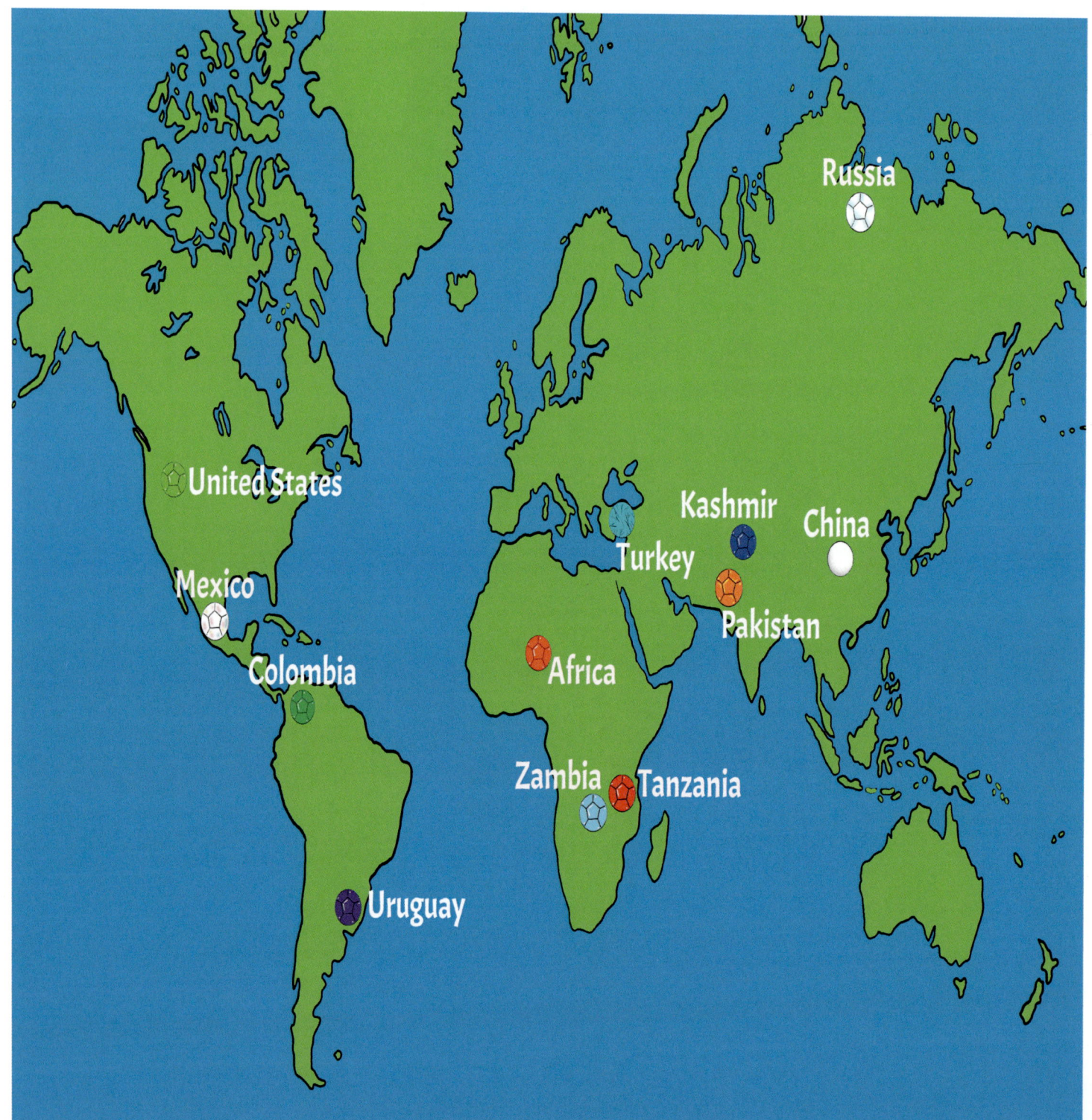

THE BIRTHSTONE BOOK

A Guide to Birthstones for Kids

by Lisa Broder

Illustrations: Bella Maher

Books by Genie Publishing, New York
Copyright © 2021 by Lisa Broder

All rights reserved including the right of reproduction in whole or in part in any form
ISBN 979-8-9850883-0-4

January	Garnet
February	Amethyst
March	Aquamarine
April	Diamond
May	Emerald
June	Pearl
July	Ruby
August	Peridot
September	Sapphire
October	Opal
November	Topaz
December	Turquoise

The first month is January.
When the year is new,
Garnet is the featured stone
In every shade but blue

GARNET is the birthstone for the month of January.
It is usually thought to be a red gemstone
however it is also present in orange, gold, and green.

Garnet is mined in Africa, Brazil, Sri Lanka, and the United States.

Message from Genie:

According to legend, garnet can bring peace, prosperity, and good health to the home.
It's been called the "Gem of Faith."

If you're born in February,
Purple is your shade.
Amethyst is a brilliant gem-
Its beauty never fades

AMETHYST is the birthstone for the month of February. It is a variety of quartz known for its fiery look and brilliance.

Amethyst is mined in Australia, Brazil , Sri Lanka, the United States,
Uruguay, and Zambia.

Message from Genie:

In ancient times amethyst was worn mostly by kings and queens because purple was the royal color.

The third month is March.
Its stone is aquamarine-
A jewel as clear as crystal,
with a hue of bluish green

The main birthstone for the month of March is **AQUAMARINE**. It gets its name from the Latin word for "seawater". It is a symbol of health, youth, and hope. This stone is also said to be a token of good luck for all those at sea.

Aquamarine is mined in Brazil, Madagascar, Nigeria, Russia, the United States, and Zambia.

Message from Genie:

Neptune, the Roman god of the sea, gave aquamarine to the mermaids.
It is said that the stone brought love to all those who wore it.

If you're born in April,
Your future has been blessed.
Your birthstone is a diamond,
Bringing love and happiness

DIAMOND is the birthstone for the month of April. It is the hardest substance on earth. Its name comes from the Greek word meaning "unconquerable". Many people think diamonds are clear colorless stones, however they come in many colors.

Diamonds are mined mainly in Australia, Russia, and South Africa.

Message from Genie:

Diamond engagement rings are symbols of the promise of marriage.
The stones are everlasting, like a love that will conquer all. The unending circle represents eternity.

April showers bring May flowers
And emeralds that are green.
May's special stone is
The loveliest ever seen

EMERALD is the birthstone for the month of May. The color ranges from medium green to dark green to bluish green. Emerald gets its name from the Greek *smaragdos*, meaning "green stone".

Emerald is mined in Australia, Brazil, Colombia, Pakistan, Tanzania, and Zimbabwe.

Message from Genie:

In ancient times people thought emeralds could help them see into the future.

The world can be your oyster
If you're born in June.
The pretty pearl has charm
Thanks to dewdrops from the Moon

The principal birthstone for June is **PEARL**. The name pearl comes from the Latin word for "tear-shaped". Pearls come in a variety of colors although usually they are white or cream.

Pearls are most often found in China, Japan, and the South Seas: Australia, Myanmar, the Philippines, and Tahiti.

Message from Genie:

Legend says that pearls were created when dewdrops filled with moonlight fell into the ocean and were swallowed by oysters.

July is the seventh month –
It's stone as red as a flame.
A brilliant deep-toned jewel –
Ruby is its name

RUBY is the birthstone for the month of July. Rubies are always red and the name comes from the Latin word *ruber*, meaning "red".

Ruby is mined in Afghanistan, India, Kenya, Sri Lanka, Tanzania, and Thailand. The finest rubies come from Myanmar.

Message from Genie:

Many believe rubies possess an inner flame that burns eternally. In the Middle Ages a ruby was believed to be a symbol of power and romance.

The year heats up in August. With the summer sun. Which stone belongs to this month? Peridot is the one

PERIDOT is the main birthstone for the month of August. It is a lime-green stone, in ancient times considered the gem of the sun. It is formed by volcanic eruptions.

Peridot is mined in Australia, Brazil, Myanmar, Sri Lanka, and especially the United States.

Message from Genie:

Peridot is said to be like the tears of Pele, the goddess of the volcano.

September's gem is sapphire,
A blue stone some might think;
But its many rainbow colors
Include yellow, orange, and pink

SAPPHIRE is the birthstone for the month of September. It is present in many colors except red. Sapphire gets its name from the Greek word *sappheiros,* meaning "blue".

Sapphire is mined in Australia, Kashmir, Kenya, Myanmar, Sri Lanka, Thailand, and the United States.

Message from Genie:

Ancient people believed sapphires gave the heavens their blue color.

If you're born in October,
The opal is your gem.
It sparkles like many jewels.
With colors from all of them

The birthstone for October is **OPAL**. Opals have many colors in them. Their name originates from the Greek *opalios*, meaning "precious stone".

Opal is mined in Australia, Mexico, and the United States.

Message from Genie:

Ancient people believed opal was made of the wonders of other gems—the rich purple of amethyst, the fire of ruby, the green of emerald—all sparkling together.

Topaz comes in many colors,
Including amber gold.
This birthstone of November
Is a beauty to behold

TOPAZ is the birthstone commonly thought of for November. It gets the name from the island Topazios, in the Red Sea. Topaz occurs in many colors: blue, gold, orange, peach, pink, red, and yellow, but most commonly it is golden yellow.

Topaz is mined in Brazil, China, Nigeria, Pakistan, and Sri Lanka.

Message from Genie:

In ancient times, people believed that topaz was colored with the golden glow of the sun god named "Ra". Topaz was also considered to increase the strength of anyone who wore it.

December has blue turquoise,
A stone unlike the rest.
Of all the wonderful jewels
Which one do you like best?

December's birthstone is **TURQUOISE**, an opaque blue to green mineral. It is named after the country of Turkey where it was found.

Turquoise is mined in the Afghanistan, Australia, India, Iran, and United States. The finest quality turquoise is found in Iran and is referred to as Persian Turquoise.

Message from Genie:

Turquoise is used as a healing stone and good luck talisman by Native American tribes. It represents life.

The practice of dedicating a special stone to each month dates back to the first century A.D. It was linked to the twelve stones in the breastplate of the High Priest of Israel and the twelve signs of the zodiac.

Made in the USA
Las Vegas, NV
05 April 2025